Earthforms

Volcanoes

by Xavier Niz

Consultant:
John D. Vitek
Professor of Geology
Oklahoma State University

Capstone
press

Mankato, Minnesota

Bridgestone Books are published by Capstone Press,
151 Good Counsel Drive, P.O. Box 669, Mankato, Minnesota 56002.
www.capstonepress.com

Library of Congress Cataloging-in-Publication Data
Niz, Xavier.
    Volcanoes / Xavier Niz.
    p. cm.—(Bridgestone books. Earthforms)
    Summary: "Describes volcanoes, including how they form, plants and animals near volcanoes,
how people and weather change volcanoes, volcanoes in North America, and the Ring of Fire"
—Provided by publisher.
    Includes bibliographical references and index.
    ISBN 0-7368-4309-4 (hardcover)
    1. Volcanoes—Juvenile literature. I. Title. II. Series: Earthforms.
QE521.3.N59 2006
551.21—dc22   2004028515

Editorial Credits

Becky Viaene, editor; Juliette Peters, set designer; Kate Opseth, book designer; Anne P. McMullen,
    illustrator; Wanda Winch, photo researcher; Scott Thoms, photo editor

Photo Credits

Bruce Coleman Inc./E.R. Degginger, 4; Masha Nordbye, 16; V&W/Philip Colla, 10
Corbis/R.T. Holcomb, cover; Vittoriano Rastelli, 14
Digital Vision, 1
Houserstock/Dave G. Houser, 8; Jan Butchofsky-Houser, 12

1 2 3 4 5 6 10 09 08 07 06 05

Table of Contents

4

What Are Volcanoes?

Volcanoes are underground **vents** that shoot out **lava**, gas, and **ash**. Most volcanoes are tall and shaped like cones. Others are flat and short. Some volcanoes **erupt** often. Other volcanoes haven't erupted in hundreds of years.

Volcanoes are located all over the world. Many volcanoes form on the ocean bottom. Some of these volcanoes grow tall enough to rise above water. Other volcanoes form on land.

◄ Hot lava flows down Hawaii's Mount Kilauea. This volcano has been erupting since 1983.

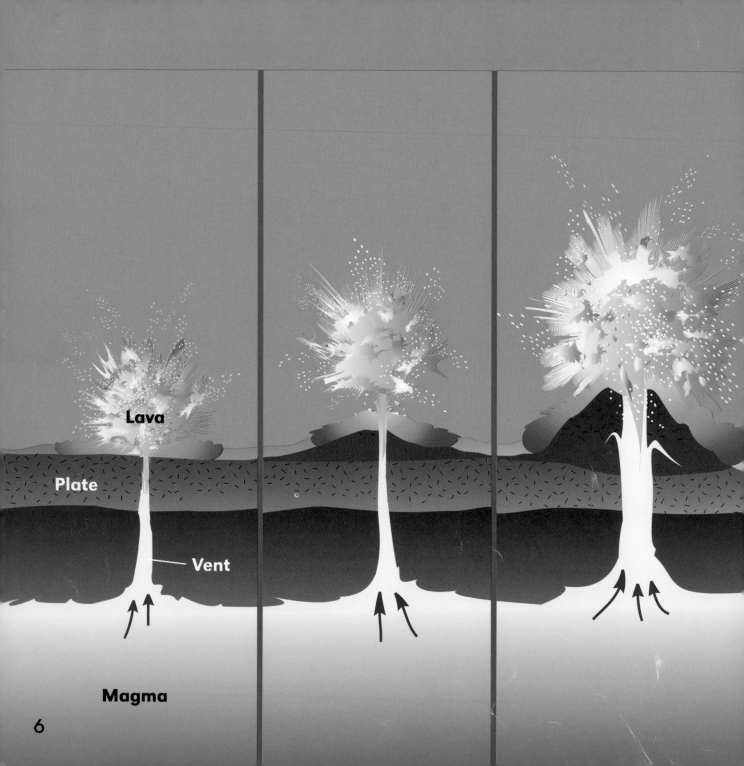

Lava

Plate

Vent

Magma

How Do Volcanoes Form?

Volcanoes form when liquid rock called **magma** breaks through earth's surface. The surface is made of huge rocky plates. Magma lies under the plates. When the plates separate, magma flows up between them through vents.

Magma that flows onto earth's surface is called lava. Lava cools and hardens. Layers of lava pile up, creating a cone or flat shape.

◀ With each eruption, lava piles up. Over time, a volcano grows taller.

Plants on Volcanoes

Ash shoots out of erupting volcanoes. It falls to the ground and adds **minerals**. Plants start growing soon after volcanoes erupt. The Ohia Lehua tree is the first plant to grow on lava in Hawaii.

Over time, plant roots break down hard lava into sand. This sand becomes rich soil. In Hawaii, moss and ferns grow just months after eruptions. Later, trees and large plants begin to grow.

◀ Plants in Hawaii's Volcanoes National Park push up through lava and grow.

10

Animals Near Volcanoes

Areas around underwater volcanoes are full of life. Lava flows from underwater vents. The lava adds minerals to the ocean. The minerals are food for tiny creatures called **microbes**. Shrimp wait near vents to eat the microbes.

Serpulid worms and large clams also live near underwater vents. Temperatures near vents can be more than 600 degrees Fahrenheit (316 degrees Celsius).

◄ White serpulid worms are found near vents in the Pacific Ocean.

Weather Changes Volcanoes

When volcanoes are not erupting, weather begins eroding them. After years of erosion, only a volcano's middle remains. New Mexico's Ship Rock formed this way.

Weather changes volcanoes, but volcanoes also change weather. Volcanic eruptions shoot ash miles into the sky. Ash can form clouds that block sunshine from reaching earth's surface. This can cause temperatures to drop. Ash can stay in the **atmosphere** for more than two years.

◀ Rising 7,178 feet (2,188 meters) high, the remains of this volcano, called Ship Rock, continue to erode.

People Change Volcanoes

People living near volcanoes need to stay safe from lava. They change volcanoes by building walls and digging tunnels near volcanoes. The walls and tunnels change the direction lava flows, so it can't destroy towns.

People put pipes deep in the ground to use heat from volcanoes. The heat is used to create steam. Steam is run through machines to make electricity. In Iceland, heat from underground volcanic activity warms homes.

◄ A bulldozer builds tall walls to change the direction of lava flowing from Mount Etna in Sicily, Italy.

Volcanoes in North America

Pico de Orizaba is one of the tallest volcanoes in North America. It stands 18,700 feet (5,700 meters) tall in Mexico. Pico de Orizaba last erupted in 1687.

Mauna Loa, in the Pacific Ocean, is the largest volcano on earth. Half of the island of Hawaii is covered by this volcano. It streches across an area of 2,035 square miles (5,271 square kilometers). Above sea level, Mauna Loa is 13,680 feet (4,170 meters) tall.

◀ About 500,000 people live around the bottom of Pico de Orizaba.

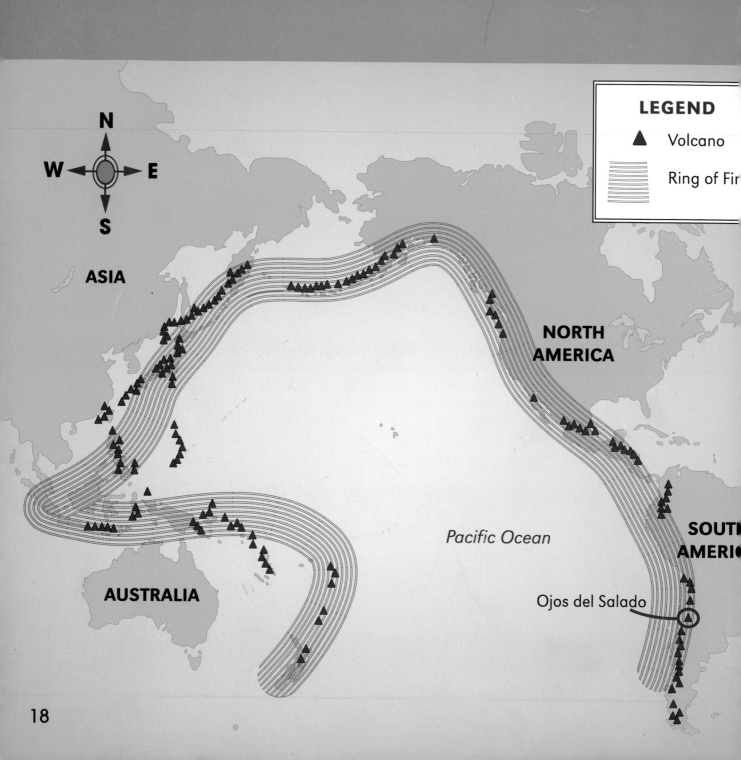

Ring of Fire

The largest band of active volcanoes circles the Pacific Ocean. This band is called the Ring of Fire.

The Ring of Fire has 75 percent of all volcanoes in the world. Chile's Ojos del Salado is one of the largest volcanoes in this group. It is the tallest active volcano in the world. Ojos del Salado is 22,664 feet (6,908 meters) tall.

◄ Volcanoes in the Ring of Fire are found on land and underwater in the Pacific Ocean.

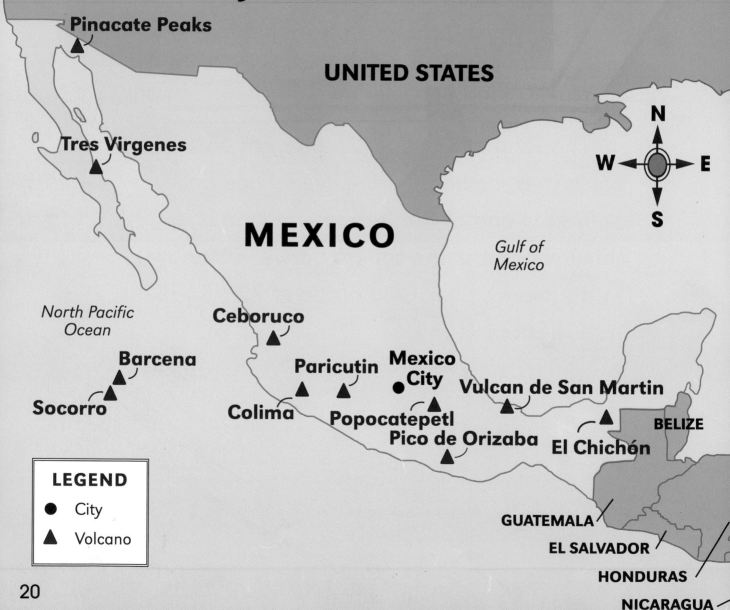

Major Volcanoes of Mexico

Pinacate Peaks

UNITED STATES

Tres Virgenes

MEXICO

Gulf of
Mexico

N
W — E
S

North Pacific
Ocean

Ceboruco

Barcena

Paricutin

Mexico
City

Vulcan de San Martin

Socorro

Colima

Popocatepetl

Pico de Orizaba

El Chichón

BELIZE

GUATEMALA

EL SALVADOR

HONDURAS

NICARAGUA

LEGEND
● City
▲ Volcano

Volcanoes on a Map

Look for red triangles on a map. These triangles show where volcanoes are located. Volcanoes are found in the ocean and on land. Volcanoes' names are usually listed next to the red triangles.

Red triangles show volcanoes that have been discovered. As the plates move, new volcanoes can form. New maps may show new volcanoes.

◀ Red triangles show the many volcanoes located in Mexico.

Glossary

ash (ASH)—powderlike material that erupts out of a volcano

atmosphere (AT-muhss-fihr)—the mixture of gases that surrounds a planet

erupt (e-RUHPT)—to suddenly burst; a volcano shoots lava, ash, and gas into the air when it erupts.

lava (LAH-vuh)—the hot, liquid rock that pours out of a volcano when it erupts

magma (MAG-muh)—melted rock found beneath the surface of earth

microbe (MYE-krobe)—a living thing that is too small to see without a microscope

mineral (MIN-ur-uhl)—a substance found in nature that is not an animal or a plant

vent (VENT)—a long narrow passage; lava, ash, and gas erupt out of vents.

Read More

Durbin, Christopher. *Volcanoes.* Geography First. San Diego: Blackbirch Press, 2004.

Lassieur, Allison. *Volcanoes.* Natural Disasters. Mankato, Minn.: Capstone Books, 2001.

Internet Sites

FactHound offers a safe, fun way to find Internet sites related to this book. All of the sites on FactHound have been researched by our staff.

Here's how:
1. Visit *www.facthound.com*
2. Type in this special code **0736843094** for age-appropriate sites. Or enter a search word related to this book for a more general search.
3. Click on the **Fetch It** button.

FactHound will fetch the best sites for you!

Index